MARC ANTHONY

A Real-Life Reader Biography

John Torres

Mitchell Lane Publishers, Inc.
P.O. Box 619 • Bear, Delaware 19701

First Printing

Real-Life Reader Biographies

Paula Abdul	Mary Joe Fernandez	Ricky Martin	Arnold Schwarzenegger
Christina Aguilera	Andres Galarraga	Mark McGwire	Selena
Marc Anthony	Sarah Michelle Gellar	Alyssa Milano	Dr. Seuss
Drew Barrymore	Jeff Gordon	Mandy Moore	Shakira
Brandy	Mia Hamm	Chuck Norris	Alicia Silverstone
Garth Brooks	Melissa Joan Hart	Tommy Nuñez	Jessica Simpson
Kobe Bryant	Salma Hayek	Rosie O'Donnell	Sinbad
Sandra Bullock	Jennifer Love Hewitt	Rafael Palmeiro	Jimmy Smits
Mariah Carey	Hollywood Hogan	Gary Paulsen	Sammy Sosa
Cesar Chavez	Katie Holmes	Freddie Prinze, Jr.	Britney Spears
Christopher Paul Curtis	Enrique Iglesias	Julia Roberts	Sheryl Swoopes
Roald Dahl	Derek Jeter	Robert Rodriguez	Shania Twain
Oscar De La Hoya	Steve Jobs	J.K. Rowling	Liv Tyler
Trent Dimas	Michelle Kwan	Keri Russell	Robin Williams
Celine Dion	Bruce Lee	Winona Ryder	Vanessa Williams
Sheila E.	Jennifer Lopez	Cristina Saralegui	Tiger Woods
Gloria Estefan	Cheech Marin		

Library of Congress Cataloging-in-Publication Data
Torres, John Albert.
      Marc Anthony/John Torres.
         p. cm.—(A real-life reader biography)
      Includes index.
      ISBN 1-58415-069-6
      1. Anthony, Marc—Juvenile literature. 2. Singers—United States—Biography—Juvenile literature.
[1. Anthony, Marc. 2. Singers. 3. Hispanic Americans—Biography.] I. Title. II Series.
ML3930.A54 T67 2001
782.42164'092—dc21
[B]
                                                              00-067665

ABOUT THE AUTHOR: John A. Torres is a newspaper reporter for the Poughkeepsie Journal in New York. He has written eleven sports biographies, including *Greg Maddux* (Lerner), *Hakeem Olajuwon* (Enslow), and *Darryl Strawberry* (Enslow). He lives in Fishkill, New York with his wife and two children. When not writing, John likes to spend his time fishing, coaching Little League baseball, and spending time with his family.

PHOTO CREDITS: cover: Paul Fenton/Shooting Star; p. 4 Yoram Kahana/Shooting Star; p. 7 Archive Photos; p. 18 Globe Photos; p. 24 Archive Photos; p. 27 Globe Photos; p. 30 Shooting Star.

ACKNOWLEDGMENTS: The following story has been thoroughly researched, and to the best of our knowledge, represents a true story. While every possible effort has been made to ensure accuracy, the publisher will not assume liability for damages caused by inaccuracies in the data, and makes no warranty on the accuracy of the information contained herein. This story has not been authorized nor endorsed by Marc Anthony.

Table of Contents

4

Chapter 1
Destiny

As singer Marc Anthony got ready to walk onto the stage, his name was announced. But the crowd did not go wild. As a matter of fact, only one person in the audience, which was made up mainly of disk jockeys, even clapped. Marc had never been so nervous in all his life.

It was 1993 and Marc was about to perform at a Latin music convention in New York City called Radio y Musica. It was virtually the first time he was singing Salsa, in Spanish, in front of strangers. Salsa is a fast-paced Latin

Marc Anthony remembers the time he was about to sing on stage and no one even clapped.

style of music filled with percussion and horns and Marc wasn't used to singing that way. Even though he had recorded Latin music before, it was mainly ballads and dance tunes.

Marc felt he was at a crucial moment in his career. Even though he was only in his mid-twenties, he considered it to be a final shot at stardom. Until that point he had been a little-known New York club singer. In fact, at the time of the show Marc was going through some rough times. He was so poor that he had to borrow clothes from a friend to wear on stage.

So it is easy to understand why Marc was so nervous. His hands trembled as he held the microphone. To relax, Marc closed his eyes and tried to make believe he was singing to his mother in the living room of his apartment.

When he was done with the song, Marc literally ran off the stage. He was so relieved about being finished that he did not realize an audience that had

For years, Marc had been a little-known New York club singer. He wanted his shot at stardom.

refused to acknowledge him just a few minutes earlier was now giving him a standing ovation and cheering wildly. People were asking one another where they could find Marc's latest recording. One of the disk jockeys who had just heard him sing had thrown that very recording in the trash that morning. He was desperately calling his assistant to get it out before the wastebasket was emptied.

Marc Anthony did not realize it at the time, but his life was about to

Long before Marc was a Latin singing sensation, he sang before small crowds in clubs around New York. Fame did not come easily.

change forever. Never again would he have to borrow his friend's clothes to appear on stage.

Just a few weeks before this career-changing performance, Marc had been driving around listening to music on his car radio. He was getting tired of the dance club scene where he would basically perform one song over and over again in the course of a night and hoped he could find something else to do. Then he heard a slow ballad called "Hasta Que Te Conoci," on his car radio, and called his manager immediately. Marc liked the ballad and wanted to record it as a Salsa song. Soon after he recorded it, he chose it as the song he would perform at the Radio y Musica convention.

It was a good choice. As Marc relaxed backstage after singing it, a producer in the audience ran up to Marc. The producer booked Marc to perform later that day on a Spanish-language television show called

"Carnival Internacional." People all over the world would hear Marc sing his song — and love it.

"That changed my life forever," he said. "I mean in one day. It seemed like years before I was ever in New York again. I was booked and booked and booked."

Suddenly this club singer, a New York-born Puerto Rican, was in demand all over the world. He soon recorded an album of Salsa music that became very popular.

Marc was beginning to make a name for himself. The big money was not quite coming in just yet, but Marc was laying the groundwork for a career that seemed to come from a fairy tale, with humble beginnings and a limitless future.

"That changed my life forever," he said.

Chapter 2
Growing Up

Marc's family moved from Puerto Rico to New York hoping to make a better life.

Marco Antonio Muniz was born on September 16, 1969 in Spanish Harlem, New York. Spanish Harlem is a neighborhood on the Upper East Side of Manhattan Island, a part of New York, where many Puerto Ricans immigrated in the 1950's. Not feeling comfortable in a new environment, and not being able to speak English, the immigrants set up the close-knit neighborhood in order to feel more secure than if they had been scattered throughout the entire city of New York.

Puerto Rico is an island in the Caribbean, rectangular in shape, that stretches for 110 miles and is about 35 miles wide. There are approximately 3.5 million people living on the island, which was a Spanish colony for nearly 300 years. The United States gained control of the island in 1898 after the Spanish-American War, and it became a U.S. commonwealth in 1952. This means that Puerto Rico enjoys some benefits from the American government while enjoying a sense of freedom as well.

But many people living in Puerto Rico don't make much money, and some leave the small island hoping for a better life for themselves and their families in America. That was why Marc's family moved to New York.

Marc's father, Felipe, was a musician.

Marc's father, Felipe Muniz, was a musician and he named his son, who is the youngest of eight children, after a famous Mexican singer. Because Marc's family was very poor, they didn't have much money for entertainment. So they would often gather at the kitchen table in their small apartment and listen as Felipe and his friends would sing and play Jibaro music all night long. Jibaro is Puerto Rican folk music, often thought of as farm, or country music.

One night, when Marc was nine years old, his father had him join a jam session that was going on. Marc loved the attention and so he stood up on the kitchen table and began to sing. He sang so beautifully and so passionately that when Marc was finished the room was silent — except for his aunt, who was crying. Marc's voice and the tenderness of the song had evoked a cherished memory for her and she could not contain her emotions.

"I almost retired when I saw that," Marc laughed. "I thought, 'I'm in trouble. I'm going to get punished.'"

Quite the contrary. Marc's family recognized his talent immediately and began encouraging him to sing. Soon, Saturday night concerts in their apartment became popular within their small circle of friends. Marc's stage was the kitchen table — until he grew too tall to stand on it!

Marc's favorite song to sing was called "El Zolsar," about a type of bird that lives in Puerto Rico.

"He loved that one song," his father said. "He could really belt it out."

But Marc was not instantly drawn to the Jibaro music or the Salsa, which were the favored styles of his father and many of his brothers and sisters. No, Marc was drawn to popular music. He loved rock and roll, rhythm and blues, as well as dance music. One of his favorite singers growing up was Billy Joel. Marc also enjoyed the music of Paul Simon, never daring to dream that one day they would be working together.

He was sort of discovered during a talent search at the age of 12. That led to his first small exposure to the music business as he worked for David Harris, who was a producer of demonstration tapes and commercials. Harris hired Marc and one of his sisters to do background vocals.

But, Marc was drawn to popular music. He loved rock and roll, rhythm and blues, as well as dance music.

By the time he reached high school, Marc knew that he wanted to follow in his father's footsteps and become a singer. So he began auditioning for just about anything he could find. The hard work and exposure paid off as Marc landed a gig as a backup singer for a wildly popular Puerto Rican teen singing group known as Menudo. The group had been around for a long time and constantly replaced members when they became too old to fit the image. Ironically, one of Menudo's members during that time period was Ricky Martin, who today is an acclaimed pop and Latin music star.

"Yeah, I worked with Ricky long before all this," Marc said. "I wrote three songs on their 'Sons of Rock' album, which was Ricky's last year with them. I produced the vocals, sang background on the album, and went on tour with them for like a month."

While Marc loved being involved in the music industry, he was hoping that one day he would feel what it was like to have adoring fans screaming for him. Despite not getting the glory of being center stage, Marc loved every minute of his experience with Menudo.

"Hey, when you're 15 or 16 years old, that's the gig to have," he said.

Marc went to a performing arts high school and studied subjects like music composition, writing lyrics, sound engineering, producing records and dance. He was setting himself up for a career in music. He was hoping it would be on a stage.

Marc became a backup singer for the Puerto Rican teen singing group, Menudo.

After his stint singing and writing songs for Menudo, Marc met a music producer known as "Little" Louis Vega. The two hit it off immediately and Vega asked Marc if he would be interested singing backup for a band he was starting called the Latin Rascals.

Marc agreed and even though he wanted to branch out into his own music career, he saw this as a good opportunity to learn even more about the industry. He also figured that working with Vega would give his career the exposure it needed.

In the early 1990s, Marc worked with a record producer named Louis Vega.

Marc worked long hours recording with the group, which specialized in club music. Weekends were filled with appearances at small clubs dotting the New York City area performing one song over and over until something else became popular. Marc loved being involved but felt that something was missing. He wasn't making a lot of money and he wasn't really performing the kind of music that he liked.

Then, in 1991, Vega received a contract from Atlantic Records and asked Marc to be his singer. That hard work had paid off. Marc was finally the frontman — or lead singer — of a group. It still was dance music and Marc would still have to work as a club singer but it was a step in the direction he wanted his career to take.

The two young men called themselves Little Louis & Marc Anthony. They recorded an album called "When the Night was Over." The album enjoyed great success in the dance-music scene and the lead song

In 1991, Marc got to record an album with "Little" Louis.

"Ride on the Rhythm" was a #1 dance hit that year. Its popularity began opening doors for the group as they started making appearances before bigger audiences than they were accustomed to.

In 1992, famous Latin percussionist and bandleader Tito Puente asked Vega and Marc to open his show at New York's famous Madison Square Garden. Marc and his friend "Little" Louis Vega had never performed before such a big crowd. Nervous at first, the two shook their fear once the music started and people began cheering. The crowd went wild for them and that was the first time Marc realized how tired he had grown of playing before small crowds in crowded clubs.

Marc went back to playing the small clubs and the group had another hit song, "Rebel," which is still sometimes played in New York dance clubs. Marc's manager told him that perhaps he should try singing in Spanish if he was tired of being a club singer. But Marc resisted until that fateful day when he heard the song "Hasta Que Te Conoci." He decided then and there that he would record it in Spanish and finally try his hand at Salsa.

Marc resisted singing Salsa, but when he finally did, it started his career.

"The song ripped me apart," Marc said about first hearing it. "I don't know why and I don't want to know why. I called my manager and asked if I could record it."

Marc signed a contract with a Salsa label and started gaining popularity. Audiences were drawn to this skinny singer with the golden voice and, more important, people starting buying his recordings.

Marc had gotten his wish. He was finally the frontman, the stage was his. There was no turning back now. He recorded two Salsa albums that were hits and began playing in front of large crowds all over the world. By the time Marc recorded his third Salsa album, "Contra La Corriente," which means "Against the Current," many people felt he was the most popular Salsa singer in the world. In fact, due to advanced sales and orders, the album earned a gold record status even before it hit the shelves.

Little did he know that his switch from English to Spanish music would eventually lead him back to his roots, back to American pop music, and help fulfill his dream.

Believe it or not, his switch from English to Spanish would help Marc get back to American pop music, and help fulfill his dream.

Chapter 4
Capeman

Pop superstar Paul Simon is known in the music business as an innovator, a person who isn't afraid to try new things. In the 1980's he combined American rock and roll with the sounds of South Africa to create "Graceland," one of the most successful albums of all time. A few years later, Simon, a native New Yorker, melded Brazilian jazz with American pop for the hit album "Rhythm of the Saints."

So it came as no surprise that in 1997 Simon decided to write a play that he hoped would capture the spirit of New York's Latin music scene. It would

Paul Simon wrote a play he hoped would capture the spirit of New York's Latin music scene.

be performed on Broadway, the famous New York City street where many theatres are located.

Simon chose to make a musical production of the true story of Salvador Agron, a 16-year-old Puerto Rican gang member who stabbed two people to death in a street fight in 1959. After his trial, he was sentenced to death, though New York's governor later decided that he should not be executed. Agron, who wore a black cape during the gang fight, became known as "Capeman" and Simon thought that would be a good title for his play.

So Simon wanted the hottest Salsa singer around to play the young Agron, the lead role in the play. Apparently Simon went into a record store and asked the clerk who the best Salsa singers were. The clerk gave him a Marc Anthony disc and said he was the one.

When he got home and heard Marc's music, Simon knew that he would be perfect for the role.

He chose to make a musical production of the true story of Salvador Agron, who stabbed two people to death in a street fight.

"They gave me two or three guys to listen to," Simon said. "I listened and I thought 'This is good. In fact, it's really good,' and Marc Anthony was clearly the best."

The next step for Simon was to convince the young Salsa star that it wasn't a practical joke. He left a message for Marc, who was skeptical.

"It was him (Simon) on the other line, asking if I could come over," Marc said. "I couldn't believe he was giving me his address."

Simon was set when he later hired Latin music legend Ruben Blades to play Agron as an older man.

The show opened early in 1998 but immediately ran into problems. Although Agron had been released from prison after serving 20 years and made headlines as a reformed convict who never committed another crime and even earned his college degree while behind bars, many people in New York still had bad feelings about him. Drama critics, who write reviews of Broadway

Paul Simon chose Marc Anthony, the hottest Salsa singer around, to play the young Agron.

shows, hated the show. There were demonstrations outside the theater by those who felt that the show glorified murder. All of these things discouraged people from buying tickets. So even though "The Capeman" had a great soundtrack and a cast that included Marc Anthony and Ruben Blades, it had to close after just a few weeks.

The public and critics did agree on one thing, however. They loved this

Marc loves to perform in public before large audiences.

singer, Marc Anthony, who was performing in English for the play.

Major record labels took notice of his good reviews. They also took notice of something else Marc did.

Just before "The Capeman" was set to open, Marc decided to throw a sort of farewell concert, since he did not know how long he would be performing on Broadway.

He became the only Salsa singer ever to sell out Madison Square Garden. That fact alone made major record labels interested in him.

This sort of star power, as well as his willingness to sing English music, convinced Columbia Records that he was a sure-fire bet for stardom.

He signed a $30 million multi-album deal with Columbia that would allow him to record either in English, his first love, or in Spanish.

Next stop for Marc? The top of the charts.

Marc became the only Salsa singer ever to sell out Madison Square Garden.

Chapter 5
Superstar

Marc's daughter, Arianna, is the subject of his hit song, "My Baby You."

While Marc was finding success on the stage, he was not as lucky in love. Marc was involved in a few high-profile relationships but just could not come up with the perfect fit he was looking for. However, a failed relationship resulted in the love of Marc's life: his daughter Arianna, who turned 7 in 2000.

So it came as no surprise to anyone who knew Marc that he would include a song written for her when his self-titled album, "Marc Anthony," was released in 1999. The song, "My Baby You," is one of the most passionate and eloquent songs on the disc.

Like many of Marc's Spanish recordings, he wrote and chose all the songs on the album carefully, making sure they reflected exactly what he wanted to say.

"I'm not out to conquer the world," he said. "It's just that everything I do has to come from the heart."

And he added, "I made an album that I'm extremely proud of. I wrote 90 percent of the songs. The melodies are

Marc received an ALMA award at the Civic Auditorium in Pasadena, California. Here he is shown with Jennifer Lopez (left) in 1999.

mine, the lyrics are mine and some of the music. Everything I wrote was heartfelt. There was no bull about it. I just closed my eyes and it poured out."

It was the first time Marc felt confident enough to write his own songs. Since English is his first language, he never felt comfortable writing love songs in Spanish.

"Spanish is a much more poetic language, especially in songs, and to capture a color or a mood in the air, the language lends itself to that more than English. It's an art form in itself," he explained.

Well, his first stab at writing Latin-based American pop music proved what a great songwriter Marc really is. He scored billboard hits with several singles released from the record including the hard-driving "I Need to Know," which made it to the Top 10, and the ballad "You Sang to Me."

The album became a big hit and suddenly the Salsa singer turned

Marc's first stab at writing Latin-American pop music was a success.

Broadway actor had become a pop star. He went on a full-scale North American tour and wowed audiences wherever he went.

He also was making inroads in another entertainment arena. Marc had become close friends with Ruben Blades during their stint together in "The Capeman," and Blades, who starred in several motion pictures including "The Milagro Beanfield War," helped Marc get a shot at the movie business.

Marc landed a role in the film "Hackers." Then he played a waiter in Stanley Tucci's "Big Night," where he was noticed by legendary filmmaker Martin Scorsese.

Scorsese tabbed Marc to play a prominent role in "Bringing out the Dead," a movie that was scheduled to be released in 2000. Marc welcomed and loved the opportunity to work with Scorsese and Academy Award-winning actor Nicolas Cage. His role as a troubled homeless man ensured that he

He is also appearing in several movies.

Finally, in 2000, Marc met his soulmate, and married Dayanara Torres.

would be asked to roles in even more films.

Marc, who had won a Billboard Music Award in 1994 for Best New Latin Artist, got to perform at the 2000 Grammy Awards for Excellence in Music. He even walked away with his own award for Best Tropical Latin Performance.

2000 was not just a banner year for Marc in music and in movies. He finally met his soulmate, Dayanara Torres, a former Miss Universe. The couple were married in May in Las Vegas and planned to buy a home in Puerto Rico. In February 2001, the couple had a son, Cristian Anthony Muniz, born in New York City.

Marc said that he plans to record more music in both English and Spanish and simply will follow where his heart leads. While other Latin pop music performers such as Jennifer Lopez and Ricky Martin seem to grab a lot of the headlines and the glitz associated with the music business, Marc just goes about his business of writing and singing songs that have personal meaning.

In fact, he sometimes gets angry when the three singers are lumped together to explain the "Latin Explosion" in pop music.

"I hate that hoopla stuff," he said. "It just puts the attention on the wrong thing, like Latin sensation. Barbra Streisand is not known as a Jewish sensation. It's not about the Latin thing for me, it's all about the music."

For Marc, this business is just about the music.

Chronology

1969, born on September 16
1978, starts performing for family members at the age of nine
1981, is discovered and gets his first taste of the music business
1984, performs with Ricky Martin for the group Menudo
1991, records an album with Little Louis Vega
1992, performs at Madison Square Garden
1993, records his first Salsa album
1994, wins Billboard Music Award as Best New Latin Artist
1997, stars in Paul Simon's "The Capeman" on Broadway
1999, records the album "Marc Anthony," which is a pop music hit
2000, May 10, marries Dayanara Torres
2001, February, son Cristian Anthony Muniz born

Index